The Gospel According to Brodie

The Gospel According to Brodie

LESSONS FROM
A BLIND LABRADOR

Jennifer Rees Larcombe

ZONDERVAN™

GRAND RAPIDS, MICHIGAN 49530 USA

ZONDERVAN™

The Gospel According to Brodie
Copyright © 1995 Jennifer Rees Larcombe

Requests for information should be addressed to:
Zondervan, *Grand Rapids, Michigan 49530*

ISBN 0 551 02985 4

First published in Great Britain in 1995 by Marshall Pickering

Jennifer Rees Larcombe asserts the moral right to be identified as the author of this work

A catalogue record for this book is available from the British Library

Illustrated by Annabel Playfair

Interior Design by Susan Ambs

Printed and bound in the United States

02 03 04 05 06 07 08 /❖DC/ 10 9 8 7 6 5 4 3 2 1

To Minty, Brodie and Candy without whose help I would never have written this book.

Foreword

When Jen told me about her ideas for *The Gospel According to Brodie* I felt very enthusiastic because I knew immediately how many it would appeal to. What she has to say is refreshing and deeply meaningful, yet like herself, full of warmth and fun.

Someone once said that 'a dog is a man's best friend'. Well that is certainly true of Brodie and Jen. Brodie has a wonderfully trusting nature. She follows Jen and likes to keep close to her wherever she can. Because Brodie is blind, there are times when Jen literally has to be her eyes. Brodie puts full confidence in her. Being blind myself, I know how important these special relationships of trust are. When I had my first guide dog I had to learn to trust her to lead me in many different situations. I was terrified at first, but as we got to know each other I began to feel I could rely on her. One day, when all the paths were covered with snow, I was completely lost. All my landmarks were gone, but my dog knew exactly where the roads were and we arrived home safely.

Unfortunately, my dog was not always as well-behaved as Brodie! On one occasion after having a nice lunch at a friend's house, she saw a cat outside. Before I knew what was happening, she leapt through the glass door into the garden wrecking the window, leaving herself completely unscathed and me with a hefty bill!

Jen relates many humorous incidents about Brodie, and they all serve to show us that life can be a tremendous adventure of faith. People believe that what you see is all that matters, but faith and trust can only be developed as we allow ourselves to take risks – to become vulnerable as we rely on others. Brodie and I have learnt a lot about this.

I was appalled when Jen told me that someone had suggested Brodie be put down because of her blindness. Just because she's lost one of her senses doesn't mean she can't have fun and enjoyment in life. I certainly do! As you read these pages I am sure that you will find many valuable insights into what makes life worth living and pointers that will help you to develop that most important and special relationship of all – a personal friendship between you and God, which is based wholly on establishing a true foundation of love and trust.

Brodie and I would like you to curl up and relax, and enjoy this really good read. We know you are going to love it!

Marilyn Baker

Introduction

I have never met M – face to face – yet we have known each other very well for nearly ten years now. Our 'letter' friendship began when she first wrote to me in 1986:

Dear Mrs Rees Larcombe

I have just finished your book Beyond Healing ... I too am stuck in a wheelchair. I'm forty-seven and have MS ... My husband is a farmer and we live right out in the sticks. I don't see many people these days. It's hard being a Christian, isn't it, when you never get to church and friends can't visit very often. Yet I know God is nearby, specially when I sit out in the fresh air ...

I was most interested to see the photo on the front cover of the book – you in your wheelchair with a little white dog on your lap. You mention her in the book so I know her name is Minty. I too love my dogs, and I find they teach me so much about my relationship with God. Dogs are so vulnerable, in spite of their loud barks and growls; they are actually helplessly dependent on their masters for their happiness and welfare. I like to pretend I can manage my own life, but really I know my happiness and welfare are in God's hands in exactly the same way.

I hope the idea of God using animals to help humans understand him better doesn't shock you but in the Bible he did use a donkey to talk to Balaam about things in the spiritual realm which Balaam was too stupid to see for himself (Numbers 22) . . .

Far from being shocked, her letter set me thinking and forever afterwards I began to see Minty, my little Jack Russell, in a totally new light. So M and I began to write to each other about our dogs and what they taught us about our faith. Sadly M rapidly became

so disabled by her MS that she is only able to scrawl a
few words on a postcard, but I know from her husband
that she enjoyed my scrappy little notes about Minty
and the things I tell her now about the lessons that my
blind dog Brodie teaches me. This book is simply a
series of extracts from my letters to M.

Dear Ell

Thank you for your lovely letter – it was such an encouragement to me. Thank you, too, for the photo of yourself. I can picture you now, sitting by your inglenook,* the apple logs blazing and the dogs luxuriating on the hearth rug beside your wheelchair.

As you will know from reading my book, we have six children and we've recently had to leave the country that we loved so much. We now live right in the middle of a town. I miss the countryside intensely and sometimes feel very stifled by the town which seems to wall me in on every side. Minty and I used to have such fun rambling for miles in the woods and fields before I got ill. Now we have to make do in the park and put up with:

> *Keep off the grass*
> *Do not pick the flowers*
> *Do not allow your dog to . . .*

Actually, I have to admit the park does make life easier for us, because the nice little tarmac paths

---

*chimney corner

which criss-cross the grass are perfect for the wheel-chair. Since we moved here Minty has learned to walk to 'wheel' instead of 'heel'!

You said in your letter that your dogs teach you about God and how you relate to him. I suppose Minty has done that for me too. Probably I've always had a problem believing that God really loves me. I know it in my head but somehow I can't feel it in my heart. I always used to think the more I could do for him, the more he would love me, and one day I'd do something really big for him which would make me worthy of his affection. Now I'm disabled I realize I never will, so I feel like a second-class Christian, useless and pushed aside. That's where Minty comes in, because she makes me see myself in a different light. Let me explain.

She was given to us by my Auntie Gerry who has been breeding and showing wonderful dogs for many years. She's even won at Crufts! She has a very beautiful dog called Pippin to whom she is devoted. When Pippin's litter was born Auntie Gerry was delighted with the pups – until she saw Minty, the runt of the litter. She was small and sickly, her legs were far too short and so bowed they resembled the cabriole legs of a Queen Anne chair. She will never be any good for breeding, but Auntie Gerry kindly gave her to us because we wanted a nice little pet for the children who were all quite small in those days.

When Minty arrived she had a very low opinion of herself, which was not surprising after being so badly bullied by her arrogant brothers and sisters. Since then her personality has blossomed but she still has that gentle, humble, undemanding nature I would so like to emulate. There is not one shred of pride in her.

Of course she really does not have anything to be proud about. She's rather an ugly little dog and she never does anything useful. Some dogs are so accomplished they can afford to put on a few airs and graces: guide dogs, for instance, sheep dogs, the huskies who pull sledges for miles across the ice caps, St Bernards who rescue people from snow-drifts and then put fresh 'spirit' into them, police dogs, sniffer dogs or even greyhounds. Minty isn't even a guard dog; if a burglar broke in here she would welcome him with a wagging tail.

But I don't keep her because she is useful to me; I keep her because I love her. I like her to be there, sharing my wheelchair, lying curled up on my bed or sitting gazing up at me with her adoring brown eyes. That's what I mean when I say she helps me realize that I don't need to *do* great things for God to be valued in his sight. He actually *enjoys* my company, yet I'm always fussing about the things I can't *do* for him instead of just *being* there for him.

Jenx

Dear M

Thank you for your letter – I'm glad you enjoyed hearing about Minty. She really is such a funny dog. If she's feeling a bit fragile for some reason she'll run along behind my wheelchair on three legs, holding one of her back legs up pathetically. People in the park stop and make a fuss of her saying, 'Poor little dog, she's got a bad leg.' They even glare at me as if I'm being cruel to make her walk. She thrives on it, but the only problem is she forgets which leg is supposed to be poorly and gives the game away by changing the limp in mid-performance!

She really is a bit neurotic. When she wants to spend a penny* she doesn't cock a back leg to the nearest lamppost or squat like any self-respecting bitch, she does a handstand on her front legs and sprays away while her two back legs wave in the air above her head!

Jene

---

*go to the bathroom

Dear M

I saw something so funny yesterday when I was out in the park with Minty. (I have a battery-operated wheelchair now which means I can get out with her by myself – which, as you can guess, I love doing.) It's a good job that she is such an obedient dog, if she didn't come when I called her I wouldn't be able to risk taking her out on my own like that. This has nothing to do with my training; it's her nature, she just loves to please.

That certainly isn't the case with a lot of dogs in the park, who rush around madly, scaring the children and making the frail and elderly feel unsafe. Their owners shout and roar their names but they take no notice at all. One of these dogs, a white bull mastiff called Hetty, really gives her owner the run-around. He's a fat little man with short legs. Come to think about it, he looks very like Hetty herself!

Yesterday I saw him galloping all round the park after her, yelling 'Hetty, come *here!*' and cursing her at the top of his voice while he waved her collar and lead in the air above his head like a lasso. Everyone was laughing at him and he was bright red with exertion – and embarrassment. Hetty is always letting him down in public and it wastes so much of that poor man's time, too. He must sometimes wonder if the dog is worth all that hassle and humiliation.

Obedience really matters if a dog-man relationship is going to work well, don't you think? I suppose the same applies in man-God relationships too. Perhaps that's why God puts such high value on it: 'If you love me, keep my commandments.' I've always thought of obedience as something which God insists on because it benefits *us* in our Christian lives. Yesterday in the park, however, I realized how much pleasure Minty's obedience gives to me, and how much misery Hetty's disobedience generates. I began to see what a personal delight (or grief) the quality of obedience – or the lack of it – must give to God.

Jени

Dear M

Thanks for the card — I'm glad you are feeling better now the good weather has come at last. I so love this time of year, when everything's new and green again. The woods will be full of bluebells now, and I *mind* so much not being able to get out in them and walk. I often wonder if Minty misses the life we used to have together before I was ill. She came to us when I was still very fit and living in the country and we used to walk for miles together through the woods.

I told you in my last letter how obedient she is, but now I come to think of it, I can remember one terrible day when that obedience was put to the test and Minty failed completely. She does have one grand passion in her life. She loves chasing rabbits. It's cats now we live in town, but her eyesight is so bad I doubt if she can tell the difference.

On this particular day, I had taken her out in the car to some woods quite a long way from our home. We had a lovely time until we came to a clearing densely colonized by brambles. Suddenly a big fat rabbit hopped across the path right in front of

Minty, who was trotting along beside me like a little white angel on a Sunday School treat. The 'angel' stopped dead. 'No Minty!' I shouted, and for one second she hesitated while temptation and devotion struggled within her. Temptation won, and she leapt into the thicket with far from angelic intentions.

At first I could hear her crashing about in the distance and barking excitedly, but soon there was nothing but ominous silence. I grew hoarse with shouting her name as terrible stories about Jack Russells getting stuck fast in rabbit holes until they suffocated came back into my mind. Finally I sat down on a tree stump and the silence in the woods grew oppressive. Where on earth had she got to? Then suddenly, far away, I heard her yelp shrilly in fear. I knew she was in trouble and that I had to do something quickly. I would have to get into the middle of that great dome of brambles somehow, yet I had no stick or handy garden shears, not even a Boy Scout's penknife.

It was a hot summer day so my arms and legs were bare, even my toes stuck out of my sandals. But because I love her so much I just plunged straight into the brambles without a second thought. However, an

hour later when I was still beating my way through those wretched prickles I was *not* feeling quite so affectionate. My skin was ripped to ribbons, my clothes were torn and so many thorns got stuck into my feet it took a week to dig them all out again. Yet when I eventually spotted her, helplessly trapped and exhausted from trying to free herself, my anger evaporated. She was covered in blood, ears torn and eyes swollen, and she looked up at me with a pathetic mixture of repentance and gratitude. How could I possibly be cross with her?

On the way home in the car I realized I was positively hurting all over, but I was just so relieved to have her safely sitting in the back, that I didn't care. It dawned on me that my discomfort was nothing to what Jesus went through to rescue me when he died on the cross. Yet so often I take his suffering for granted and forget to thank him for loving me that much.

While I'm still on the subject of Minty's overwhelming temptation, I must tell you about the funniest time when Minty's disobedience caused her deep humiliation. Years ago we were walking a section of the Pennine Way while we were on holiday with the children in Yorkshire. Minty saw a rabbit in the distance and, in spite of our shouts, she took off like a bullet. She did not realize that a cattle grid was between her and her prey. The rabbit knew about cattle grids – Minty did not. The rabbit ran round it, but Minty, thinking she had outwitted the rabbit by taking a short cut, ran right into it. Her short front legs went down between the bars, leaving her back legs waving helplessly in the air. She did a magnificent somersault and finally landed on her back right in the middle of the grid. It took her so long to extricate herself that the rabbit must have been home in its burrow with the kettle on long before she had regained her dignity. We laughed at her so much she looked offended for the rest of the day.

We used to have such fun on holiday together in those days. Probably life isn't so good for Minty now I'm disabled. I can't take her on walks like that any more, and no one else has the time these days. I can't expect my home help to cook up the special little bits of liver or fish that she used to enjoy, so she has dried pellets instead, which taste like cardboard. I thought perhaps she might lose her love for me, feeling that dogs usually only love their masters because they feed and exercise them. Minty enjoyed rambling round 'rabbit country', of course, but now I can't take her she doesn't fuss, perhaps because her greatest delight is just *being* with me. She doesn't have any personal agenda beyond her desire to please me and stay close to me. She really loves me because I'm *me* and not for what she can get out of me.

Most of the time I'm not like that with God! How often I want him for what I can get out of him in the way of perks and special favours – instead of loving him for himself alone. I suppose it's easy to love him when he answers our prayers instantly and showers us with endless good things. Yet last winter, when I was so unwell, I began to realize that our real devotion for him shows when we go on loving him even when he hasn't done what we wanted him to do. Perhaps real friendship with him begins when we can answer the questions: Is God there for me, or am I there for him? Is he twisted round my little finger, or am I twisted round his? Is it just cupboard love I have for him, or the kind of lifelong commitment which some dogs develop for their owners? 'I'll love you just the same if you give me a bone or a worming pill, take me for a walk or leave me in the car. I'm yours entirely, whatever you do!'

Jane

Dear M

Happy Christmas!

I'm afraid this is going to be a shortie, as my fingers are not working too well at the moment. I've been in hospital in London for weeks and I'm only just home. It's been a vile patch this time. It was horrid up there, too far from home for the family to travel up to see me very often. I missed them all terribly, but do you know what? I missed Minty more than any of them. Sometimes at night in hospital I'd half wake up and feel for her with my feet, only to discover she wasn't there. A desolate feeling. I must confess I had a bit of a battle with my faith too, and the inevitable 'whys' and 'buts' seemed to build a wall between me and God.

Apparently Minty missed me too. She went right off her food and Tony says she looked thoroughly cross the whole time I was away. She must have thought I'd abandoned her for ever. When I finally came home (after a ghastly long journey in an ambulance) she didn't run out to greet me with her usual wild yelps of delight. In fact, she wouldn't come near me at all for the first hour, but stood in the corner of my bedroom, looking at me with sad reproachful eyes. Then, when she was sure no one was looking, she hopped onto the bed and slithered sheepishly towards me, as if to say, 'I thought you didn't love me any more – all those weeks you were away. Sorry I got so cross with you.' Finally she went to sleep snuggled up against my knees, just as if I'd never been away. It must be hard for dogs. Their limited canine intelligence must often leave them puzzled by their owners.

Next morning a friend sent me a card. There was no picture on it, just the words 'My Father, I don't understand you but I trust you.' For some reason it helped me profoundly.

Jene

Dear All

Something terrible happened last week, but it really taught me a good lesson. About tea time on Tuesday Minty suddenly had a massive haemorrhage. I could see she was going into shock and when Tony rushed her up to the vet, he didn't hold out much hope for her, and said it was caused by this horrible virus Parvo. I must have forgotten her jabs.*

'We'll keep her here and see she doesn't suffer,' he told Tony. Well, she may not have suffered, but I did! During the endless night which followed I kept thinking, 'I can't lose her, she's the joy of my life!' And really she has been, always making me laugh at the funny little things she does. Then I thought, 'But should I have allowed a dog (or anything else for that matter) to become "the joy of my life?" Isn't that what God wants to be – the centre and source of all my happiness?'

Yes I *know* he gives us the gift of dogs, children, friends – all kinds of things, but they should only be surface joys. The real, deep-down 'joy of life' must

---

*shots

come from knowing him because that's the only 'joy' which is permanent. Dogs and children, youth and health, they're only lent to us for a short time. We have to hold them lightly on an open hand rather than clutching them tightly with a clenched fist.

The next morning when we rang the surgery the vet said Minty had made a remarkable recovery and by Thursday she was back home, a bit wobbly and thin but ecstatic to find me again. Phew! a close shave. How will I cope when she does die, I wonder? That reminds me of a poem I learnt as a child. I think it was by Rudyard Kipling:

> *Brothers and sisters I bid you beware*
> *Of giving your heart to a dog to tear.*
> *There is sorrow enough in the natural way,*
>
> *From men and women to fill our day,*
> *So when we are certain of sorrow in store*
> *Why do we always arrange for more?*

Jean

Dear All

I feel dreadful that you had to read all about what's been happening to me in a magazine. I wanted to write and tell you myself, but I felt so odd about it all that somehow I couldn't find the right words. Perhaps I feel guilty because I am so well now and you are still in your wheelchair.

You ask, 'Is it *really* true?' Well yes, it *is!* After eight years of hospitals, painkillers and being officially registered as a disabled person, I am now totally well and full of energy. And the whole thing happened so suddenly, I'm still reeling with surprise.

On 13 June I was speaking in a church near Guildford, sitting in my wheelchair and in a lot of pain. At the end of the service a girl called Wendy prayed for me. She's a new Christian and had never prayed out loud in her life before. I'd been prayed for hundreds of times, as I guess you have been, but perhaps the time wasn't right before. I didn't 'feel' anything as she prayed, I just knew I was well. I stood straight up and walked about. That was two months ago and I haven't sat in the wheelchair ever since. From that very moment I've felt totally well, pain-free and full of energy.

I feel so choked up as I'm writing all this to you because I can't understand why God should do this for me. I used to ask 'Why God?' so often when I was ill, but this has left me with far more questions than ever before! I think if I'd earned this gift of health in some way, I'd feel better about the whole thing. But it certainly wasn't my faith, or anything I *did,* not even a particular person or a recognized 'holy place' that I went to – it just happened.

You'll be asking, 'What does Minty make of all this?' Well, she doesn't approve at all! After so many years of always seeing me sitting down, she simply can't relate to a standing, walking me and she's completely disorientated. She got so used to having me always at home and *there* for her, but now, half the time I'm out shopping, swimming or playing golf and she isn't asked to come too. She *hates* it! I'm not sure if dogs can have nervous breakdowns, but I really think Minty is getting depressed.

The first morning after it all happened I got up early, about five in the morning, and took her out for a walk. Actually I wanted to go out alone before the streets were crowded to see how far I could walk without lots of people staring at me. Once we were in the park I went mad and ran through the dew on the sloping lawns making criss-cross patterns with my footprints. It was glorious, but Minty ran along behind me looking distinctly puzzled and not a little cross. Her patience snapped when I jumped on to a low wall and balanced along the top of it (you know how children love walking on walls – just to see if they can). Minty had had quite enough by then and she exploded with a volley of indignant yaps while she leapt repeatedly in the air snapping in the direction of my ankles.

I suppose it's no wonder she's disturbed really, because I must look and smell the same as ever but suddenly I appear to act like a totally different person. That bothers the children too, but at least they have a bit more chance of understanding what's happened to me.

It's ironic really, but now I *can* take Minty for walks again, she refuses to come. I suppose she's got lazy pottering round the park or even riding along on my lap in the wheelchair. And of course I want to walk *miles* every day, now I've got the chance to do so. My sons say I go too far and too fast for them, so I guess poor Minty feels the same. She's taken a deep dislike to my new walking boots and every time she sees me putting them on she lies on her back with her legs in the air! She also hates me doing my aerobics before breakfast each morning and hides morosely under the armchair until I've finished. One morning she suddenly darted from cover and bit me!

After that explosion of anger she seemed to go into a complete decline. She's so mopey now her head hangs down one end of her body and her tail hangs down the other (like Eeyore in *Winnie the Pooh*). She just lies in her bed all day, even refusing her favourite minced liver. Tony says she's not putting it on this time, she really *is* ill. Pippin, her mother, died of cancer at just this age, so perhaps we're going to lose her soon. She is nine after all.

Even our holiday in Devon didn't help – but it was the best summer ever for me! One day I walked twenty-two miles all alone along the South-West Coastal Path. Needless to say no one else would come with me! In the eight years since I could last walk alone like that, the world has changed a lot, and you do hear about horrible things happening to women.

I would feel so much safer if I had a dog to protect me. Minty, even if she were well, would never do that! So I'm beginning to think that, should we ever lose Minty, I'll get a large, black, fierce-looking dog, preferable one who loves long-distance marathons. Of course I would *never* consider having another dog until Minty is no more. It wouldn't be fair, would it? She's been such a good friend for so many years.

Jenx

Dear M

Thank you so much for ringing last night. It was good to hear what your voice sounds like after 'knowing' you for so long. You've still retained your Scottish brogue! It's so attractive, specially when it gets mixed up with the Welsh lilt you must have picked up from your husband.

Thank you for being so concerned for poor little Minty. Yes, she really is in a bad way, she's so thin and listless now. I'm praying she'll die in her sleep one night because I simply couldn't take her to the vet for the last time – and leave her there.

On Thursday my friend Grace came over to see me from Mayfield (the village in the country where we used to live). We went for a walk on the common together and she asked me what I liked most about this new healthy life of mine. I told her it was being able to get out into the countryside and walking for miles all on my own. But I also told her how nervous and vulnerable I feel and of my determination to buy a big black dog to protect me. She laughed and said, 'You ought to have Brodie.'

Brodie is a black Labrador puppy who is proving to be a bit of an embarrassment to poor Grace. Lois, Grace's daughter, works for a vet in Crowborough. On 15 June (just two days after my healing) a bitch was brought in for an emergency caesarian section because she had developed toxaemia. The puppies were valuable because both parents are very aristocratic and have mile-long pedigrees. Apparently 'mum' is a triple champion, but had left it a bit too late for a first litter. Sadly most of the thirteen puppies were DOA and the rest had eye problems caused by the toxaemia. The vet decided not to let them live, and anyway the bitch was too ill to be bothered with them. Lois, who was assisting him, has a very kind heart (like her mum) and asked if she could try and rear the two strongest-looking pups by hand. That night she came home with them in the pocket of her overall.

She fed them every two hours with a dropper – even at night. One of them, Brodie, who is a greedy little thing, gobbled it down and is doing very well. The other one didn't seem to take to tinned puppy milk and died a fortnight later. Brodie is now seven weeks old and thriving – except that she is totally blind.

Lois and Grace are now facing a big problem. They've lost their hearts to her, but can't possibly keep her. Grace has been 'minding' her during the day while Lois is at work, but Grace is a teacher and term starts next week. They have to find a home for Brodie before then. They've asked all over the district but no one wants a blind puppy, not even one with an impressive pedigree. Several people have even suggested the best thing to do is to have her put down.

I know you will understand what I mean when I say, 'That makes me livid.' Having lived for eight years as a handicapped person, and been blighted by the prejudice of the 'well' section of the human race and their low opinion of the disabled, I really 'feel' for that puppy. All through those years, when I was just a number on a DSS file, I hated feeling I was written off by society because I was not able to do *exactly* the same things as they could.

When Grace had gone home, we all sat round the tea table that evening and talked about nothing but Brodie. All the children feel we should have her. After all, we've discovered as a family that having a handicap does not mean a person cannot live a very full and satisfying life. Tony said, 'I suppose she could protect you on walks just as well as a sighted dog, so long as you always kept her on a lead.' So on Sunday we're going to see Brodie. We have decided that if she comes towards us we will know she is meant for us, but if she takes no notice or doesn't seem to like us much, then we'll forget all about it.

My only concern is Minty. Should we really introduce a bouncy puppy and spoil her peaceful dying? Tony says the shock will kill her instantly. In a way, I would rather that happened than the horror of the last trip to the vet's. Please pray we'll know what to do.

Jене

Dear All

Brodie is going to be ours! We went over to Grace's on Sunday afternoon and Brodie was out in the garden. As soon as she heard our voices and footsteps she came lolloping across the lawn towards us on her ridiculously large puppy feet. Her tail is disproportionally large too, and it was wagging her whole body. Because she has been hand-reared she's totally used to humans. She gave us such an exuberant welcome we all knew we had to have her. Tomorrow we are going to fetch her. Please do pray Minty won't be too upset.

Jane

Dear M

Sorry I haven't written for so long but I never realized puppies were such hard work. Worse than babies really, except that you don't have to change their nappies* – even though you wish they could wear them sometimes.

Another miracle has happened in our family. Far from being upset by Brodie's arrival, Minty has come back to life! She positively froze with horror for the first few hours and sat in her bed with hair standing up along her back like an aggressive scrubbing brush. We waited for the terrible moment of conflict but it never came. Minty watched Brodie blundering into all the furniture with an increasingly puzzled set to her ears. She must have sensed that there was something wrong with Brodie. When the inevitable happened and the puppy bumped into Minty's bed she didn't leap out and execute vengeance, she simply pecked at Brodie like a mother hen cuffing an erring chick.

---

*diapers

Brodie's blindness does make her very docile and lacking in confidence and there is something very endearing about her which appeals to Minty – just as it does to everyone else. We've never let Minty have a litter because of her bow legs so perhaps there is some repressed need within her that is now being met by this puppy. Already Brodie is far bigger than she is, but Minty bosses her around, licks her clean and yaps firmly if she misbehaves. Minty has a little bell on her collar and Brodie has now taken to following the tinkling sound and lumbering along behind Minty when we are out in the park. So not only has Minty taken on the role of nursemaid, but now she is a guide dog for the blind as well! All this has given her something to live for. She's regaining weight and her coat is looking sleek again. Her illness must have been psychosomatic after all. Brodie has certainly given her a new lease of life.

The other day we took Brodie out for the first time. She hadn't had her jabs because she wasn't quite fourteen weeks then so we didn't want to risk the park. Parvo, the virus which once nearly killed Minty, is very prevalent in town parks apparently. So Duncan (our middle son) and I took the dogs out to a big field in the country. We thought we could begin to train Brodie to come when we called her name. She did very well, thanks to a stock of dog biscuits in our pockets.

Brodie also followed the sound of Minty's bell and soon they were running all over the field. All went fine until Minty wanted to spend a penny. Did I ever tell you that she does so while doing a handstand? Of course Brodie didn't know she had stopped in order to perform and blundered into her, right in midstream. Minty went somersaulting, legs over head, right onto her back. She looked most put out and nipped Brodie's back leg until she yelped. How we laughed!

There were some wonderful blackberries in the hedges round that field and all the time we were there an elderly lady was busily picking away while her husband snoozed in a deck chair nearby. They didn't seem to like dogs much so we kept away from them. We were about to leave for home when this couple came towards us, arm in arm, clutching two ice-cream cartons brimfull with blackberries – not to mention a picnic basket and the deck chair. Brodie loves people, even the non-doggie ones, and hearing their voices she ran eagerly towards them. Because we know she's blind we are used to her floundering into our legs, but of course these people obviously expected her to 'look where she was going'. They just kept on walking, ignoring her completely, and suddenly, to our horror, we saw Brodie right in between the elderly gentleman's legs. In a desperate attempt to save himself from falling he pulled his wife down as well. They both landed in a sprawled heap with Brodie somewhere in the middle and black-berries flying in all directions.

We ran up apologizing profusely while the old man sat glaring, red-faced and indignant. 'I'm terribly sorry,' I explained, 'but our dog's blind.'

'So am I!' he snapped.

'We've lost all our blackberries too!' said his wife. We offered to pick them up, only to realize that Brodie was wolfing them up like a vacuum cleaner. She'll eat anything, she's so greedy. 'Don't bother!' said the old lady, 'I wouldn't fancy them now your wretched dog's slobbered all over them!'

Duncan and I slunk back to the car, mortified with embarrassment, but I'm afraid the giggles got the better of us eventually. Minty sat on the back seat look-ing like a disapproving governess all the way home.

Jene

Dear All

Life with Brodie continues to be hectic. We have decided to join Minty in taking her 'upbringing' seriously, so we went to the library and borrowed a book by Barbara Woodhouse on training puppies. There don't seem to be any books on teaching *blind* dogs, but obviously obedience will be paramount or Brodie will walk into all kinds of danger. She's already learnt the word 'Careful!' Every time I see her rocketing towards a lamppost in the park or a closed door in the house I shout 'Careful!' She only had to bang her nose a couple of times to learn what the word means! Now it checks her almost in mid-air.

She's so greedy I don't think it will be hard to teach her other words or tricks either. She always comes when I call her name because of the biscuits in my pocket, and she learnt the word 'sit' in five minutes because I bought some doggie chocolates. To be fair, I think she does have a natural desire to please and be 'on the right side of me'.

Teaching her to walk to heel is also easy because, without her sight, she feels safer walking behind me and following the sound of my footsteps. She does so well that I can now let her off the lead in the park and she'll follow me very confidently.

Of course she does get confused when there are lots of people about and the footsteps lead in all directions. The other day I stopped to talk to a friend and she hurtled off quite happily behind a strange man thinking she was still with me. She was on the other side of the park before I saw what had happened. By then she had realized her mistake. Poor Brodie, she looked so forlorn, but quite sensibly she sat down to wait until she could locate me. I could see, even from that distance, that she was listening. She puts her nose in the air and cocks her ears in a particular way when she is trying to pick up sounds and work out where they are coming from. She was probably sniffing as well, of course. I was worried that at any moment she might take off to 'look' for me in the wrong direction – the busy High Street – so I started to call her name as I hurried towards her. The park was full of people because it was a fine Sunday afternoon, and I never dreamed she would pick out my voice from the general hubbub. But she came straight towards me, unswervingly, right across the width of the park, like a remote-controlled toy car.

Didn't Jesus talk about his sheep being able to distinguish his voice from that of the thief who broke in to steal them (John 10)? But hearing his

voice isn't always that easy, particularly when you think you've lost him. Perhaps you never have that experience, but I often do. Sometimes I feel *exactly* like that forlorn puppy sitting on the path, lost and confused in the middle of swirling crowds of strangers. I just can't think where God's got to! I lose the *feeling* of his presence and I can't seem to hear his voice through the Bible any more. Church is boring and fellow Christians irritate me no end. It usually happens when I've 'followed the wrong footsteps' because they seemed, at the time, to be leading somewhere rather nice. You know what I mean? Other interests or relationships taking God's place in the centre of my life.

Whenever these horrid 'abandoned by God' patches hit me, I usually seem to panic and think I'm finished as a Christian and that I have lost him for ever. I dash 'in the wrong direction', asking lots of people for help, and land up 'in the High Street' with so much conflicting advice I'm totally confused and discouraged. If only I would stay still, like Brodie, and wait until I could hear his voice again. God spoke to Elijah when he was going through a 'dark night of the soul' too. He spoke in a 'gentle whisper' which put Elijah right back on course, but not until he was willing to 'stand still' long enough to hear it (I Kings 19:12).

Sorry about all that, but it helped me so much. Balaam's ass speaks again! Anyway, back to Brodie's training programme. The puppy book suggested that when we take her out to 'do her business' we repeat the word 'quickly' while she performs. The idea is to teach her to perform to order, and I must say Brodie got the hang of the word with embarrassing speed.

I was walking with her through the park last Friday afternoon and we were passing the bowling green. It's the pride of the Tunbridge Wells Parks Department and is kept to perfection. Mr Miller, the groundsman, was walking back and forth behind his lawnmower leaving precise diagonal lines behind him as he went. He didn't wave and was concentrating so grimly that I guessed he was preparing for the last big match of the season. (The bowls club members take the game very seriously.) Minty was off after a squirrel (she'll never catch one, but it keeps her so happy thinking she will) and for once Brodie was lagging behind. 'Come on Brodie, *quickly!*' I shouted without thinking. Tony says it was coincidence and not obedience at all, but whatever it was it was extremely embarrassing. She ran straight onto the bowling green and deposited a huge mound of 'you know what' right in the middle. I wished I could sink under the turf as I tried to scoop it all up with two laurel leaves. It was a good job Brodie is blind – at least *she* was spared the look on Mr Miller's face. 'Disgusted of Tunbridge Wells' describes it perfectly!

The next day I discovered the remains of the puppy training book in Brodie's bed. She had chewed it to pulp and I couldn't help thinking 'good riddance!'

Jene

Dear M

I'm glad my last letter made you laugh! Brodie certainly seems to be providing us with amusement, but she's also teaching me a lot. I seem to be going through rather an odd patch lately. In fact, I've christened the way I feel the PHIT Syndrome, which stands for Post-Healing Identity Trauma. It probably sounds ridiculous, but I really don't know who I am any more. It's four months now since I walked away from my wheelchair and *nothing* has ever been the same from that moment. I feel bad telling you that – it sounds as if I'm not grateful. Of course being well is lovely, but change of any kind is always stressful, don't you think? Even when it's change for the better. And absolutely everything in our lives has changed.

Everybody I meet seems to say to me 'What are you going to do now you're well?' They all make different suggestions: 'Help us with play group . . . Take on a Sunday School class . . . Do the rugby match teas . . . Run the Brownies . . . Stand for the PTA committee . . . Collect for the jumble sale . . .' I'd love to do all these things but I've a house to run and lots of children to feed. After so many years they like having a *real* mum to do things for them again. Even with all this new-found energy there's a limit to what I can fit into each 24 hours. But if I say 'no' to people, they get offended. It all makes me feel so stressed, and last Sunday I realized why.

We gave a huge tea party for all the family and lots of friends as well. Brodie loved it — at first. She wanted to 'talk' to everyone at once and was the centre of attention because she is still so adorably puppyish. Everyone wanted to play with her, and she did her best to please them all at once. But there were just too many voices, all calling her from different directions; urging her to play with this, chew at that, come here, go there, sit, beg, lie down . . . Poor thing, she looked utterly confused and it all got far too much for her. So she sniffed her way over to my chair, crawled underneath and stayed there for the rest of the afternoon. Sensible dog! I thought, 'I can't please everyone at once either, or respond to all their conflicting demands and suggestions. It's only my "owner's" opinion that should matter to me, so I'd better do a bit more "sitting under his chair" until I feel safe again and my peace is restored.'

All the same, it *is* hard to know just what God wants us to do, isn't it? If only he'd put a collar and lead on us and *make* us walk to heel! But I suppose we aren't just dogs to be ordered about. As Jesus said, 'I no longer call you servants, because a servant does not know his master's business. Instead, I have called you friends . . .' (John 15:15) Yet I'm sure he wants us to depend on him as completely as our dogs depend on us. But just lately I seem to have a tension over that too. Perhaps it's just another part of that PHIT Syndrome. You see, I'm going to have to start earning some money somehow, because naturally we've lost all the disability benefits and pensions I used to have. We just won't survive financially if I don't do my bit. But suppose I can't get a job? And Tony's even talking about giving up his career in teaching to spend the rest of his life telling people about God. I'd love to do that with him, but where would the money come from to pay the bills?

All these worries kept on going round and round in my head, like a hamster on an exercise wheel, until once again the dogs helped me see things in proportion. Grace popped in for a coffee the other day. Brodie never forgets her and she went wild with delight. Once she'd settled down, I started doing my 'hamster wheel' stuff and pouring out to Grace all my woes and worries. She listened for a bit and then suddenly pointed to Brodie and Minty lying peacefully asleep by my chair. 'Those dogs need all kinds of things to keep them healthy and happy: the right kind of food at the right time, water, warmth, worming pills, vaccination jabs, exercise, a warm dry bed, training, encouragement, toe nails clipped, flea powder. You name it, they need it, right? Yet, in spite of all these different needs, why are they lying there so relaxed?'

'Because they know I'll give them what they need when they need it,' I replied. I was beginning to see what she was getting at, but she persisted.

'And why will you do that?'

'Because they belong to me so it's my responsibility to see they get what they need,' I replied. Then I added, 'And I happen to love them both rather a lot.'

Grace was right, of course. God loves me and Tony billions of times more than we love the dogs, and because we have given our lives to him, it is *his* responsibility to provide for us. We don't let our dogs get thin and almost starve before we bother to feed them; they don't even have to whimper for their supper. So it stands to reason God will do an even better job of looking after us. 'If you then, though you are evil, know how to give good gifts to your children, how much more will your Father in heaven give . . .' (Luke 11:13)

Jenz

Dear All

Poor Brodie! She had a nasty learning experience yesterday when I took both dogs for a walk down the valley from Otford to Shoreham. At one point the footpath crosses a field full of sheep, so both dogs were on their extending leads. I find those leads maddening when walking two dogs at once because they keep criss-crossing the strings, or run round my legs until I'm wound up so tightly I can't walk. Brodie was in a skittish mood that day and as I was untangling myself for the hundredth time she grew impatient. Pulling the lead out of my hand she set off at high speed with it bouncing over the grass behind her. I could see she was heading straight for the electric fence, so I yelled 'Careful!' but she was not feeling obedient that day and took no notice.

She hit the wire at full tilt and the shock lifted her right off the ground. She shrieked and began leaping about in all directions. This caused the trailing lead to catch in the fence, tethering her close to the live wires. The more frantically she danced about, the more shocks she received. I dashed up and did my best to extricate her but she hasn't really learnt to trust me yet and probably thought I was responsible for giving her the shocks. Every time she twisted away from me she ran back against the wires again.

The noise was dreadful, particularly when Minty ran up to join in with loud bossy barks. By this time poor Brodie was quite hysterical. Suddenly Minty lost patience and, nipping up behind her, bit her hard on the rump. That did the trick. Brodie was so surprised she stayed still long enough for me to undo her lead and pull her away from the fence by the collar. They say the best cure for hysterics is a slap on the face, but perhaps a bite on the bottom does just as well!

Jene

Dear All

Sorry I seem to be writing so often these days, but life with Brodie is far from dull. So much happens that I don't want you to miss.

Sad to say, Brodie's training programme hasn't been going too well this week. She's developed a grand passion for chewing up baskets. It all began with the waste-paper basket one evening when we were out. Next day she 'redecorated' my shopping basket with thousands of small teeth marks and finally she 'had her way' with Tony's panama hat. He used to wear it when he was gardening (in the good old days when we *had* a garden).

Her 'cravings' were funny – at first, but when we came home from church on Sunday we found she had eaten Minty's bed! We had recently bought her a new little wickerwork basket complete with pretty frills and a blue cushion. A bit ridiculous perhaps, but it was going cheap in a sale. She looked so sweet curled up in it, like a baby in a crib. When Brodie had finished with it the whole thing was a jagged wreck. She had eaten the wickerwork right down to the base, ripped the bedding to bits and even swallowed the blue silk ribbons.

We were furious and Minty looked incensed. She stalked over to Brodie's bed and sat there with outraged dignity written all over her face. She refused to come out until the next morning, not even for her supper, and Brodie was left to sleep in cold discomfort on the hearth rug. The next day Brodie's punishment was complete when all the basketwork she had swallowed made her 'quicklies' very painful indeed!

The other bad habit she has developed is jumping up. She only does it because she loves everyone so much and wants to show it with every part of herself, but of course most people prefer alternative expressions of affection, particularly when her paws are muddy. The other day a newspaper reporter rang to ask if she could do a story about my healing. I wasn't very keen to go over it all again, but she was a bit pushy and said she was coming on the next train from London. I was so worried I phoned Tony at work and asked him what to do. 'Just say, you're sorry, but you don't want to talk to her after all,' he suggested. 'And don't even let her in the door.'

It sounded so easy and it probably would have been without Brodie. As soon as the doorbell rang she 'hurried up all eager for the treat', like the little oysters in *Alice in Wonderland*. She was obviously far more pleased to 'see' the reporter than I was, and, because I had to open the door in order to say my piece, she expressed her love in her usual exuberant fashion. Unfortunately the reporter was wearing one of those very flimsy Indian skirts and Brodie's puppy claws are still very sharp. The skirt ripped from top to bottom. I was mortified! How could I send the poor girl back to London in rags and with her underwear in full view? So I felt obliged to ask her in, make her some tea and give her a full-scale interview. When Tony came home he felt obliged to give her £20 to buy a new skirt. She finally went home very pleased with herself indeed.

After that we felt we really *must* stop Brodie jumping up. We remembered that Barbara Woodhouse suggested (in the book which Brodie ate) that a mug of cold water thrown into a dog's face soon stops it jumping up. Great thought that, but the trouble is I never seem to have one handy when Brodie decides to be loving. Then I hit on the idea of keeping a water pistol in my pocket. The boys have an excellent one which holds a good quarter of a pint. The next time I took Brodie to the park I armed myself with it. She will jump up on anyone we meet and I felt grimly pleased at the prospect of stopping the habit for good and all.

The first people we met were a very nice couple with little boy. 'Oh what's the matter with your dog's eyes?' they chorused in unison. As I stopped to explain Brodie began leaping up. 'No! Brodie!' I thundered, and whipping the pistol out of my pocket I let her have its contents at point-blank range. The water came out with such force it went right up her nose and she sneezed, coughed and retched most theatrically. The 'nice' family were profoundly shocked at my cruelty and went away muttering things about the RSPCA. I slunk home not thinking very kindly of Brodie – or Barbara Woodhouse for that matter.

Jean

Dear All

    I keep storing up more funny things to tell you. Sometimes I laugh so much as I write I steam up my glasses completely.

    I think what amuses me most is the interaction between my two dogs and the way they contrast with one another. Minty, for instance, is a very fussy eater. She has to be tempted with nicely presented titbits before she will deign to eat anything. Even when it's liver or best butcher's mince she picks at it slowly and delicately, more like a cat than a dog. Brodie, on the other hand, will gobble down anything, whether it's edible or not. The other day she devoured at high speed a pile of rubber bands. The consequences were hilarious the following day when she did her 'quickly', but I'd better not describe that!

    Brodie is so much more confident now, and when we're out she'll trot behind Minty with her nose up and tail high. No one, seeing her at a distance, would ever guess she's blind. Just occasionally the 'joys of motherhood' pall slightly for Minty. Being followed all the time suddenly irritates her so she deliberately runs towards a tree. Then, just at the last moment, she does a quick side-step, like a Spanish bull fighter, leaving poor Brodie to plunge head-on into the obstacle. She certainly knows Brodie is blind!

When she doesn't have Minty to follow, Brodie manages surprisingly well, feeling her way by lifting her front paws high and stepping very carefully, rather like a horse doing a dressage exercise. I'm teaching her to respond to several key words and she's becoming more like that remote-controlled car all the time. Obviously 'Careful!' is the most vital word in her vocabulary, but when I see her approaching a steep bank or flight of steps I say 'down, down, down' and down she steps, quite confidently. The same applies to 'up, up, up' of course, but her best party trick is 'go through'. We often walk across country and naturally encounter lots of stiles or fences. Minty scrambles through or even 'flies' over the top but that is a bit beyond Brodie. So, at the sound of 'go through' she'll flatten herself to the ground and feel for the gap with her nose, then through she'll wriggle. Sometimes, of course, she has to go over the top of a wall and that means leaping down on the far side into what must feel to her like dark emptiness. (You're supposed to 'look before you leap'!) But if I say 'go through', she knows it's safe to jump because, at last, she is beginning to trust me.

I'm always scared of doing new things and God seems to be asking me to do plenty of them lately. I wish I could 'go through' at his command as confidently as Brodie does! If only I had her kind of 'blind' trust.

Of course it's a lot safer to trust God than a human owner, as poor old Brodie discovered to her cost recently. It was one of those clear, crisp autumn days you have to seize and savour before being swamped by all the wet, grey, foggy ones to come. I took the dogs to Bartley Mill, a lovely place not too far from Tunbridge Wells. There are some good walks by the river which winds away from the mill through the valley. The one thing you *must* do when walking a blind dog is concentrate because you do have to 'think' for them. But that day I forgot about Brodie completely because my mind was on an article I'm trying to write.

We were approaching a wooden bridge over the river. Minty was in one of her 'off duty' moods and scampered on ahead leaving Brodie lagging behind. I simply did not realize the danger for Brodie as I began to cross the bridge, absent-mindedly calling her to follow. She ran trustingly after me, but missed the bridge by no more than a few inches and somersaulted into the river below. It was very deep water with quite a strong current and the banks were high and steep. I panicked. I would quite happily have jumped off the bridge to save her until I realized that, like most Labradors, she is an excellent swimmer. A sighted dog, however, would have made straight for the bank. Brodie had no way of getting her bearings so she simply swam round and round in circles.

In the end it was Minty who saved the day, once again. By running downstream about 150 yards to a place where the banks were lower, and skidding down through the undergrowth to water level, she stood on the little muddy shore and began to bark loudly. Brodie heard her and started swimming towards the familiar sound. I took Minty's hint and ran along the bank calling Brodie's name. It wasn't long before she was shaking herself violently and making us almost as wet as she was. Moral of that story? Never trust a human, particularly if they happen to be a writer!

Good job God never stops concentrating on us. I suppose our faith in him develops little by little through the small things in life, so when the great big crises hit, we know where to run. Apart from my lapse at Bartley Mill, I think that is how it has been with me and Brodie. The other day her trust was really put to the test.

I took her for a walk on the common quite early in the morning. Minty wasn't with us because she'd had a little operation to remove some lumps on her tummy. On the way home we have to cross the main Eastbourne road. It's very busy, but there is a pedestrian crossing with metal barriers on either side to force people to stick to the official crossing. As we stopped by the kerb,* and Brodie did her 'sit' routine, I noticed a road-sweeping lorry* parked on the far side of the road. It was one of those huge things, with revolving brushes underneath and giant vacuum cleaner hoses to suck up all the rubbish. I thought it had broken down, but I was wrong. Just as we were half-way across the road it suddenly started up its engines. The noise was terrific as the brushes whirled

---

*curb
*truck

and tins and grit clanked as they were ground up in the monster's stomach.

Brodie went berserk with fright. She jerked the lead right out of my hand and careened madly all over the road. I could see cars approaching from both directions but she was trapped between the barriers because she could not see the way out through the gaps at the crossing. Of course she instinctively ran *away* from the alarming noise, but that meant she was running straight towards the approaching cars. I thought she was heading for certain death.

There was only one thing to do. 'Brodie, come!' I yelled. I was standing right beside the road-cleaning lorry, so to reach me she had to run right up to the very thing that was making her so afraid. It was a real crisis in our relationship. Was her trust for me stronger than her fear of the terrifying monster? For a horrible moment she stopped still, undecided, while the cars drew nearer. Then she ran straight for my legs and, grabbing the lead, I leapt for the gap and the safety of the pavement.

That afternoon, I spoke with a friend who has cancer. She's facing major surgery as soon as a bed is available and she's terrified – who wouldn't be? She kept on saying, 'But surely if God can heal you, Jen, he can heal me. So why let me go through this frightful operation?' I didn't have any answers for her – there aren't any, are there? But later I thought perhaps God does sometimes ask us to go right up to the very thing we fear. He doesn't always take it away, but, just as I called Brodie, he asks us to walk right up to it. Just before Brodie crashed into her 'monster' she discovered I was already there, waiting for her. She found me in the middle of her terror – ready to keep her safe. I'm convinced my friend will find God will do exactly the same thing for her. 'But God is faithful, who will not suffer you to be tempted above that ye are able; but will with the temptation also make a way to escape, that ye may be able to bear it.' (1 Corinthians 10:13 AV)

Jenx

Dear All

    This morning I woke at five to face a busy day. In the dark I groped with my foot for my favourite slippers – and couldn't find them. Cursing Brodie I went down in cold bare feet to make a cup of tea. Splat! I stepped in something unspeakable at the bottom of the stairs. I was too sleepy to realize what it was until I'd spread it all over the hall and dining room. Half an hour later I'd got it all up with masses of kitchen paper and a bucket full of pine disinfectant – not to mention more cursing. I had to scrub my feet too, because 'it' had oozed between my toes! As I finally reached for the kettle – splat! I stepped in a huge puddle which I had failed to see on the kitchen floor. I could cheerily have committed murder by that time, but Brodie was nowhere to be seen. Minty was pretending to be asleep in her bed, with a look on her face which said, 'Well, really! I never did that kind of thing when I was young!' Brodie's bed was empty.

    Now Barbara Woodhouse says it's no good getting mad with a puppy unless you *see* it doing the foul deed, because they have no memory. That's what *she* says, but Brodie remembers all right! I suddenly caught sight of the tip of her black tail sticking out from under the kitchen table. She usually greets me so ecstatically when I come down in the mornings you'd think I had been on an extended voyage to the moon. So she *must* have known she'd erred and fallen from grace to be hiding from me like that.

I made my tea at long last and sank down in my prayer chair. It's just a big old armchair, rather worn and sagging a bit (like the rest of us), but I always sit there in the mornings to be quiet with God for a while. I was sipping my tea with my eyes shut (it never bothers me, talking to God like that) when suddenly something leapt at me with quite astonishing force, covering me with scalding tea. I said some very unholy words that should certainly never be part of a Christian's morning devotions and discovered Brodie, trying very hard to pretend she was small enough to be a lap-dog. She gazed at me with adoring eyes (or should I say sockets?) and then nuzzled her nose into my neck. It was as if she was saying, 'I've been very bad, and I'm sorry, but I know you still love me anyway.' How could I possibly go on being cross? So I propped my Bible up against her rump and let her stay where she was.

I know you're thinking I'm just about to say, 'Isn't it good that God forgives us when we repent?' Well I'm not. I have too big a problem over that. When I've done something I'm ashamed of I 'hide under the kitchen table' because I feel I don't deserve his favour. If only I found it easier to take a running jump onto his lap and accept his love and forgiveness.

Jene

Dear All

I'm so furious, I must let it all out somehow. You'll understand, so here goes.

The other day in the park a lady came up behind Brodie who had her head down, sniffing something interesting by the path. 'Oh what a beautiful Labrador,' she gushed and reached out a hand to fuss her. I hastily said, 'Brodie, friend,' so she turned round to respond in her usual affectionate way. Then, of course, the lady saw her face. The eyes she should have had have atrophied; one lid has been stitched up and the other has almost closed. I suppose they do look a bit odd, but the women recoiled from Brodie as if she were grotesque. 'How horrible!' she exclaimed. 'You ought to put her out of her misery.' Then two days later we had a letter from someone else saying she thought we were cruel to keep a 'defective dog' and in her opinion it would be kinder to have Brodie put to sleep!

As I sit here writing to you, I can see Brodie playing in the park with Richard (our youngest son). She's having a wonderful time chasing the sound of his voice and leaping all round him, barking in delight.

She has the most enormous capacity for enjoying life and she looks so beautiful out there in the spring sunshine. Her coat gleams with health and her head is a perfect shape with ears set just right. Why call her 'horrible' and ugly when a thousand things about her are beautiful and only one is not? Why write her off as 'defective' when her body works wonderfully except in one small area? Yet, I suppose we write off human beings like that too, for just the same stupid reasons.

Far from being defective, I think Brodie's disability makes her even more useful to me. I wanted a dog for company but also for protection. Because Brodie is blind she *has* to stay close to me when we're out, instead of going off to do her own thing – exploring smells or chasing cats. So, being blind makes her better company than a sighted dog, but it also makes her a better guard dog because of her phenomenal hearing and memory for footsteps or car engines. No one she doesn't know could ever sneak round this house undetected, and if a stranger comes up behind us while we are out walking she barks ferociously. Unless, of course, I say 'Friend!', then she relaxes. And there's another thing – her disability keeps her out of trouble! Minty is developing into a real pain because of her ambition to catch a cat, squirrel, rabbit or anything at all, providing it moves. I had a golden retriever once, called Rupert, who had to be shot because he chased sheep. That will never happen to Brodie, I'm glad to say – she never chases anything for obvious reasons.

Maybe our weaknesses can be turned into assets, if we want them to be. As St Paul once said, 'When I am weak, then I am strong.' (2 Corinthians 12:10)

Jene

Dear All

Thank you for Brodie's birthday card, back in June. She's doing so well and enjoyed her first summer holiday with us in Devon. We went straight down to the beach as soon as we arrived. It was hot and sunny and we were tired after travelling most of the night so we all lay snoozing while Brodie sniffed and scratched about among the pebbles and driftwood. Minty sat stiff and erect, and looked sedately cross. She *hates* beaches and getting sand between her toes.

'You know, I'm sure Brodie is *eating* these pebbles,' said Richard.

'She *couldn't* be,' I replied. 'They're too big.' They were almost the size of hens' eggs, well pullets' eggs anyway. 'She might chew them a bit,' I added sleepily, 'but she'd never swallow anything that size.' I was wrong. Frankly, Brodie must have the stomach of a goat.

That evening the fun began. First she was sick and out shot eleven pebbles and quite a considerable quantity of seaweed. Then things began to happen at the other end. We felt it was expedient to take her for a long walk along the cliff path in the sunset. We set off hurriedly, after giving Brodie a pint of warm milk with half a bottle of cooking oil and some sugar mixed into it. Yuk! but she drank it. What a walk that was! Over and over again she had to stop and 'lay' another clutch of 'eggs'. You'd have thought she was a hen, except that it's impossible for any chicken to lay twenty-six eggs in one evening! She was fine after that, but every time we went along that particular walk, we saw the little piles of white pebbles lying beside the path and laughed until we cried.

Brodie and Minty are such good friends now, so long as Brodie remembers her place in the family's pecking order. In Minty's opinion that is at the very bottom of the pile while she, of course, is right at the top.

Jenx

Dear Ell

Sorry I haven't written for so long. I've started a letter so often, but I wanted to tell you about something which is just so painful I couldn't make myself put it into words before. We've lost Minty. I feel a bit of a fool really, shedding so many tears over a dog, but how many human friends would be prepared to offer so much love for so many years for so little in return?

Surely the most difficult thing about the death of a dog you really love is that not many people understand or even acknowledge your grief. When a human member of the family dies there's a funeral, and everyone gathers round to help you through the worst with cards, bunches of flowers and the cotton wool of their sympathy. But when you lose a dog people merely shrug and suggest you buy a new one — as if someone like Minty could be replaced from the pet shop down the road! Of course *real* doggie people understand completely, and that's why I'm writing to you.

It happened one evening, back in October. Tony and I were going out to supper with some friends but both the dogs were standing by the door with their back legs crossed. They obviously needed a walk urgently, but I felt a mess and wanted a quick bath so Tony said he would take them. He went off down the front steps with an extending lead in both hands – and that was the last I ever saw of Minty.

We have a new by-law in the park now: you *must* keep your dog on a lead or you're fined £200. It's such a relief because it seems to be part of the cult image for some young men to have a large, savage-looking dog in tow these days. The dogs are as vital an accessory to their outfit as a handbag is for a bride's mother. Tony had hardly gone more than 200 yards along the path through the park when Minty caught sight of one of these guys and his Alsatian. It's a huge creature and has been terrorizing the park for some time now. In spite of her odd legs and diminutive size, Minty always felt she had to protect Brodie from other dogs, particularly large ones. So, as usual, she began to bark ferociously.

The Alsatian bounded towards her, yanking the lead out of its owner's hand. Minty submitted immediately by lying on her back and screaming in terror, but the huge dog pounced on her, crushing her rib cage in its jaws. While the owner stood by and did nothing, it tossed her into the air and carried her in its teeth like a baby rabbit. Tony was still holding Minty's lead, but he was hamstrung because of Brodie. He certainly did not want her to get involved. Anyway, things like that are all over in a moment. When he finally forced the dog to let go, all he could do was scoop Minty up into his arms and run with her back to the house.

She was still alive but unconscious so he wrapped her warmly and drove her to the vet's. I was still lying in a bath full of shampoo bubbles, and anyway he did not want me to see her like that. Apparently she opened her eyes briefly on the vet's table. Just before she died she looked up at him, her way of saying goodbye perhaps. When I finally came out of the bathroom Brodie was standing there bewildered, waiting for me outside the door. Duncan was sitting on the floor, holding Minty's collar and lead. It must have been about then that they rang to say she had died a few minutes before. *Oh* how I wish I could have been there for her! I've regretted that wretched bath ever since.

I dreaded Minty's death for years, and often wondered how I would cope with it, but when the time came I felt totally calm. Mechanically I rang the friends who were expecting us, told them we were a bit delayed, and then joined Tony at the police station. As I heard him giving his statement I felt totally detached, as if he was talking about someone else's dog. In fact, as I went to bed that night I felt quite proud of myself for reacting so well. Actually I wasn't reacting at all. When you hit your thumb with a hammer it doesn't hurt at all – at first. I suppose we were in shock really. I floated around in a daze for several days, feeling all disconnected, staring into space and forgetting what I was supposed to do next. I kept 'hearing' Minty barking or 'catching sight' of her trotting about the house. It's odd how your imagination plays tricks on you at times like that. But I didn't cry, I didn't even feel sad, and I flatly refused to talk about Minty or the details of the tragedy.

In the end Tony, who is very wise, decided we must both let some of this pain out in some way, so he made me go with him to the place where it happened. I think I read somewhere that when people have gone through some terrible trauma, or their relatives have, it sometimes helps them to go back to the place where it happened. Somehow it helps them to face up to their feelings. Tony found the very place on the path and we stood there while he described exactly what had happened. I think he *needed* to do that, for his own sake as well as mine. I still had that sense of being disconnected until I looked down and saw brown bloodstains on the path at my feet. Suddenly the shell I had grown round my emotions cracked and finally burst.

Strangely, the first thing I felt was anger. I was so angry I amazed myself! I was furious with the Alsatian, its owner, Tony for not acting faster, and myself for wallowing in a bubble bath. I was even angry with Minty for barking in the first place. I didn't just 'think' angry, I raged and roared out loud. When it was all spent I cried and cried. I think Tony was a bit watery too, but I still had enough restraint left not to look.

Finally, he suggested we say a prayer asking Jesus for the comfort he promises to those who mourn. I'm sure he wouldn't exclude dogs from that beatitude. But I did feel, as Tony prayed, that we would have to forgive that man and his Alsatian if we wanted the comfort, so I muttered 'I forgive you'. I honestly thought that I had, but perhaps real forgiving from the heart isn't quite that easy. Every time I look out of my window and see the two of them going along the paths in the park where Minty and I walked together for so long, I feel all tight in my chest, and have to start forgiving all over again. I'm beginning to realize that forgiving is something you have to go on working at day after day; it's not a decision you make once and that's the end of it.

We were not sure what to do about letting the police prosecute the man. After all, it didn't seem a very forgiving thing to do. On the other hand, various people told us their dogs had been attacked by it, and two cats had been killed. Suppose next time it goes for a child? Anyway, we went ahead and the case came up at the beginning of January. Now we can't think why we bothered really, because the owner was given a suspended sentence and was ordered to keep the dog under control in the future. The dog was still free to terrorize the park. I felt so cross there was no fine to pay, it showed my motives for taking him to court had *not* been very pure after all. Obviously I wanted revenge.

Maybe real forgiveness can only happen when we ask the Spirit of Jesus to come into the middle of the pain and anger and change our hearts, making them forgiving and loving like his own. That's easier said than done, particularly when the person you are trying to forgive has no idea how much they have hurt you.

One Sunday, before Christmas, I went to church too furious to sing a single hymn! I'd been out with Brodie in the park when we met this man and his dog head-on. I'm so afraid of anything happening to Brodie that I turned round and hurried away. Because the court case was coming up, he shouted abuse and all kinds of insults after me at the top of his voice. I fumed all the way to church, and kept on saying to God, 'How can you expect me to forgive that man? You look for some signs of repentance from us before *you* forgive, so why should I forgive someone who never said he was sorry, not even at the time?'

During the sermon I thought a lot more about it all – and I'm afraid to say I never heard a word the preacher said. Isn't it the *willingness* to forgive which counts? Maybe the other person's reactions don't really come into it. God is always *willing* to forgive us, but we lose out when we don't receive his forgiveness and cash in on all its benefits. Then, of course, I remembered Jesus on the cross when he said, 'Father forgive them . . .' Those soldiers who were hammering nails through his hands were not sorry one bit. In fact, they were laughing and mocking him all the time, adding insult to injury like the man in the park. Poor little Minty! How strange that such an odd, unassuming little dog should cause me to think such deep and profound thoughts.

I bet you're thinking, 'And how has all this affected Brodie?' The answer is, 'badly.' Really, it was Brodie's reaction that I found almost more painful than anything else. At first she was totally lost without Minty, who, of course, had been her 'eyes'. I had tried hard to train Brodie to follow my footsteps but really she much preferred to follow the bell on Minty's collar. The three of us must have travelled hundreds of miles together, over the downs and moors and through the woods. Minty always led the way with Brodie right behind her, literally nose to tail, and me, slightly redundant, trailing along behind. In addition, having Minty to follow meant that Brodie could run and play like any sighted dog, but without her she only had me.

At first she refused to walk at all. For the first two weeks I had to pull her forcibly by the collar into the park, grunting in protest. It was like hauling a big, black, reluctant elephant along behind me on a string. If any other dog came near us she was obviously terrified – and if they were big, so was I! Just when I was ready to give up the daily effort of lugging her round the park she suddenly seemed to accept that Minty had gone. Although I was a poor substitute, she was going to make the best of me. So she cheered up, relaxed and began to follow my footsteps very well indeed.

I hate trite little clichés, but the one which says 'there's a silver lining in every cloud' does happen to be true in this case. There is a great deal of difference between having one dog and two. One dog and its owner can become such a partnership they almost know what the other is thinking. Somehow it's harder to relate to two dogs at once. In the old days, when there was only Minty, we were inseparable. I had Minty's undivided attention and love. Once Brodie arrived, however, Minty became so busy licking her big black puppy into shape that our relationship was never quite the same again. As Brodie grew up she never really learnt to rely on me while she had Minty. I've found it deeply satisfying to have Brodie looking to me now for everything. Instead of lying next to Minty in some patch of sunshine or in the warm corner by the radiator, she comes and finds me and lies down as close as she possibly can.

I was talking to a doctor friend of ours outside church the other day. Like me, he's recently had his fiftieth birthday. We were commiserating with each other, when he said, 'After fifty it's nothing but loss, loss, loss — all the way down the hill.' Taken aback I asked him what he meant. 'Well, your children are likely to leave home, there's a high probability that your spouse may die or walk out on you. Statistically you are likely to lose your health and mobility — to some degree anyway — so you lose the activities or sport you've always enjoyed. You retire from work, younger people are drafted on to the committees upon which you liked to serve, and soon your arthritis even stops you playing bowls!'* I told him I thought he needed Andrew's Liver Salts and a stiff walk by the sea, but I guess there was a grain of truth in what he said. We *do* lose our props as we get older. The only thing we can

---

* British game

be sure of keeping for ever (if we want to) is our relationship of love and trust with God. As I've watched certain friends growing old I've realized that the more the props vanish, the deeper that relationship with him has a chance to grow.

Incidently, I hope as I get older that I'll always have a dog. They keep you physically fit because you *have* to walk them every day, but they make you laugh too and that does more for us human beings than most other activities.

Jene

Dear All

It's been ages since I last wrote. I am sorry, but life is so different now and packed full of so many things. I laugh sometimes when I remember how worried I was just after I was healed, not being sure what God wanted me to do with my new-found health. He knew *exactly* what his plans were for me but I was just about as blind as Brodie herself. There's a verse in Isaiah 42 which says, 'I will lead my blind people by roads they have never travelled. I will turn their darkness into light and make rough country smooth before them. These are my promises.' (v 16 GNB) He is certainly leading me along some roads I've never travelled before, and most of them seem to be motorways!

These days I'm driving all the time to speak in churches, at conferences, and at outreach events in clubs and pubs all over the place. After not driving for eight years, I'm certainly making up for lost time. I was so frightened the first time I drove on the M25 (soon after I was healed) that I was stopped by the police – for going too slowly! I've got my confidence back now, but all the same I'm very glad to have Brodie's company. Women are so vulnerable alone in cars but Brodie would ward anyone off. I do miss Tony, though, and the children (only Duncan and Richard are left at home now); however I'm always back for some of each week to do the washing and fill up the larder.*

Brodie loves the car, which is just as well because I often have to stay overnight, sometimes in three or four different beds in one week. I don't usually take Brodie in with me. For one thing, people don't always like dogs (how odd of them!), but also she takes a long to time to settle. In a strange house she will spend an hour or two sniffing and feeling her way round the furniture, exploring the stairs and getting a sense of the layout of all the rooms. When she has built herself a complete mental map of the place she never bumps her nose on furniture again (so long as no one moves anything, of course). All this prowling about and sniffing can be most annoying if you want to sleep after a long drive, so I leave her 'on guard' in the car with plenty of blankets and she's fine.

---

*pantry

She is now a much-travelled dog, and in between meetings we can always take time off for a good walk together. There was one week recently when we hiked over a Welsh mountain, trotted sedately through the streets of Bath, rambled on Dartmoor and finished up running on the Sussex Downs near Beachy Head. 'That's no place for a blind dog!' I almost hear you saying, but I didn't take her too near the edge! Anyway, Brodie and I have a varied life and these days it's certainly a question of 'have dog will travel'. Perhaps the thing we both like doing most is visiting schools. Teachers are always trying to encourage children to read instead of watching so much television, so they like to invite authors to go in and talk about their books. I always take Brodie in with me, and she's the star of the show every time.

Jenr

Dear All

Thanks for the cassette you recorded for me. It must be much easier for you to communicate with friends like that. You asked me if I thought your speech is more slurred than it was a while back. Perhaps it is, but don't worry about it because you are still perfectly distinct, and you sound as if you're delightfully tipsy!

You were asking if Brodie misses Minty at all now. I don't think she does, but I do! I keep thinking I'm over her death, but then I'll open a drawer and find a photo of her, or I'll discover some white dog hairs under furniture I don't often move. Brodie and Minty were always so funny in the mornings. They used to come into our bedroom while we were drinking our tea and lick each other clean. We called it their 'morning ablutions'! It was hilarious to watch them – one so big and the other so small.

Now Brodie still comes into our room at the same time. She pushes the door open with her nose and in she comes with a huge smile on her face. And she *does* smile, her mouth turns up at the corners and her tail goes mad with delight. When her head comes round the door, we'll be sitting up in bed with the tea tray between us and our Bibles propped up on our tummies. First she goes round to Tony's side (somehow she always recognizes him as 'pack leader') and she puts her paws up on the edge of the bed to lick whatever bit of him she can reach. Then she comes round to repeat the operation with me. She seems to feel the need to touch base with us in the morning, as if to say, 'Hello, I'm here. What have you got planned for me today?'

In a way, I suppose we are doing the same thing with God as we sit there talking to him in the mornings: 'We're here, we love you. What's on today?' This morning, when she came in as usual, I couldn't help wondering if God waits with as much anticipation for us to 'push open his door' at the beginning of the day.

Tony always says the same thing to Brodie as he pats her good morning: 'Yes, you're beautiful and we think you're very lovely.' I'm sure she knows that's what he's saying too. And again, that's what we need to hear when we read the Bible. God tells us over and over again in there how special we are to him. We all need to know we're loved and wanted

and valued. So many human beings – and dogs for
that matter – must wake up every morning and have
no one to tell them they're beautiful or worth anything at all. God never ever wanted it to be like that.

Jene

Dear M

I hope your holiday went well. It isn't always that easy going away complete with wheelchair and all the paraphernalia. I remember it only too well. We had a good summer with another lovely holiday in Devon. No 'stone swallowing' this time!

Greed remains Brodie's greatest vice, however. She will sit for hours under the dining-room table just on the off chance that a tiny crumb will fall to the ground. Her hearing is so acute, she knows instantly when something does fall. When we're all at home there's not a lot of room under our table, with so many knees and large feet, so we make Brodie sit in her bed. Now don't go thinking she's so obedient she just stays there because we say so – not when there's food around anyway. Her bed is in the corner of the dining room, so all we have to do when we want to keep her penned in is to lean a piece of wood across the corner. It isn't attached to anything, so she could easily push it over with a flip of her paw, and it is not very high so a sighted dog would jump straight over it. But Brodie sits in the corner and waits patiently for someone else to let her out. The flimsy barrier which is keeping her from what she wants so much would be quite useless if she only she realized her own power.

Recently I've been learning a lot about the power and authority God gives to us through prayer. I guess I'm a bit like Brodie: too content to sit passively hoping for some miraculous intervention from someone else – or even God himself – instead of pushing by faith against the barriers which hem me in. If only we *really* appreciated how much power God unleashes when we pray. I guess none of us would ever bother to rise from our knees.

Jenx

Dear All

Brodie and I have been having such a lovely time down here at Alfriston this autumn. I've taken some time off travelling to write a new book, and in order to get some peace she and I are staying here in this lovely little village in the Sussex Downs. Some friends have a studio room at the bottom of their garden and they have let me 'camp' in it while writing the book. No telephone, no television, no cooker,* no bath; just a tap, a kettle, a desk and a bed. Bliss!

We both miss Tony a lot, so we go home at weekends, but I find it increasingly hard going back into town with all the noise and bustle. It's so peaceful here, just miles of downs and open sky. When you love the countryside but have to live in town you cope, but something dies inside you, like an oak leaf shrivelling up in the autumn. The Downs look so lovely this time of year and we walk miles every day.

Brodie is a remarkably placid dog, totally undemanding. She'll lie motionless in her bed for ten or twelve hours on end so I can work away undisturbed.

---

*oven

When she wants something she gets up and stands at my elbow. She doesn't whine or yap, she just looks at me – well, she looks as if she's looking anyway! Sometimes it's fatal for me to stop in midchapter, I lose my chain of thought, so I just have to keep going to the end. This can mean ignoring her for ages but she still doesn't fidget. She just waits until I'm ready. Some dogs pester and fuss and want their demands met instantly, but being able to wait quietly is such a lovely quality.

I was wondering yesterday if God doesn't look for the same characteristic in us. We want our prayers answered 'right now!' but sometimes there is a very good reason why he can't grant our requests for a while. He's not busy writing a book of course, but I sometimes think he's doing a giant jigsaw puzzle – he may have other pieces to fit into the picture first. While Brodie is waiting beside me I know she wants something. Surely prayer is simply standing before God in an attitude of waiting, expecting him to do something but being happy to leave the time and method up to him. 'I wait for the Lord, my soul waits, and in his word I put my hope. My soul waits for the Lord more than watchmen wait for the morning.' (Psalm 130:5-6)

Jene

We're grandparents! I've just come back from Canada, where I've been for the last month, and was there when Sarah's baby, Hannah, was born. A wonderful experience, I can tell you.

However, I missed Brodie. She would have enjoyed experiencing all the raccoons, skunks and groundhogs with me. I never thought I'd actually *see* animals like that in real life. Of course, she wouldn't have 'seen' them even if she'd been with me, and I doubt if she would have enjoyed smelling the skunks! She probably didn't miss me much because she has become so fond of Tony. I think they kept each other company.

Changes are in the wind for us. I can hardly believe it, but I think we may be moving back to the country again soon. We've been stuck in the middle of town for ten years now, and I'm a 'Wellington boot' person at heart really. However much you walk in the country, it's not quite the same somehow when you're 'just visiting'. You can't watch the seasons changing in a particular hedgerow or know the mammals and birds in a wood until you can visit them often and spend long lazy hours watching things grow. While we had so many children at home we needed a big house, but soon we'll only have Richard left. It's ridiculous to live on four floors, with three flights of stairs and six bedrooms. So we thought, if we are 'going small' why not 'go country' at the same time? The town seems to suffocate me sometimes and I yearn for a garden again – and more time to potter in it.

The trouble is, we're so excited about the idea of moving, there is a danger we could dash off and buy something in quite the wrong place. Job-wise it doesn't matter where we live so long as we're near the motorway system. So, should we go into the wilds where the prices are low or stay here in Kent and get something not so nice for our money? Once again, it's been hard to know what God wants us to do, and in our excitement we've already nearly made a bad mistake. We found a gorgeous house with a lovely garden. Our offer was accepted and everything was going smoothly when we discovered the fields all round it had been bought by a big housing development company.

You've probably already guessed but there's a Brodie reason for me telling you all that. You see, while I was away in Canada she did get into a bad habit. Whenever she hears a certain drawer opening and her lead being pulled out, she goes absolutely berserk with excitement. She wants to go out for a walk so badly but she hampers my preparation by running round my feet, leaping in the air and barking until my ears ring. In fact, she behaves more like a badly trained puppy than a dignified dog of four years old. It really isn't like her and it makes clipping on her lead impossible because she won't keep still long enough. So I'm being very firm indeed. I tell her to 'sit!' and then I refuse to put on her lead until she is completely motionless and relaxed. Even her ears have to flop before I'm satisfied. It takes a lot of self-control for her to calm herself right down like that, but it's the only way I can give her the walk that she wants so badly.

As I went through this new routine the other day I suddenly realized that is how God wants *me* to be at this time of excitement, anticipation and change. While I'm yelping with tension and running round in excited circles trying to catch my tail he can't guide me at all. We must both sit still until he's ready to lead us out to wherever he wants us to go. 'Be still and know that I am God.' (Psalm 46:10) Apparently there is another way of translating that verse: 'Relax, take a deep breath and acknowledge that I am here.' I'm finding that a very comforting thought at the moment.

Jenni

Dear M

Sorry this is only a postcard. Brodie sends love. We're here on holiday in Devon again. Cliff walks and splashing in the sea. We've found the loveliest house for sale. Miles from anywhere and really old. Stream in the garden! Love J.

Dear All

Disappointment bordering on despair! You remember that mill house I told you about in Devon? We were sure we were going to buy it and move down there. It was so beautiful and I could just see Brodie sitting on the lawn by the stream or curled by the inglenook on a cold winter's night. Everything seemed fixed and then, right at the last minute, all the plans folded like a carefully constructed house of cards when someone opens the window. All we were left with were our dreams in a scattered heap!

Why? God seemed to be holding that mill house out to us. Then, just when we were about to take the gift from him, he withdrew it completely leaving us with nothing in its place. Most odd. We've sold our house here and must be out of it in January, but where should we go . . . ? Sorry! I'm at it again. When will I learn from Brodie? I really don't know how God would deal with me if he didn't have dogs to help him!

The day after the sale fell through I put Brodie's lead on her as usual after she'd had her breakfast and started towards the park. She was settling down to a nice steady jog, with the prospect of at least half an hour of bliss ahead of her, when I suddenly realized what a lovely day it was. 'Why not go down to Alfriston and walk my disappointment off on the Downs?' I thought. If I did my chores at high speed I could be off and away by eleven. Obviously I didn't want to waste time so I turned on my heel and went straight home. Brodie, of course, had no way of knowing about the fun I was planning for her later. All she knew was that the pleasure I had promised was suddenly being taken away for no reason she could understand. She followed me back into the house with ears drooping reproachfully and a limp and wagless tail. With a sigh she sat down inside the front door and waited there while I dashed round with the Hoover. She was obviously disappointed but she stayed by the door because she simply couldn't believe I would let her down. I longed to explain but, although she understands a lot of words, her vocabulary does not run to, 'Wait a bit longer and I'll take you for a fabulous four-hour run in the hills.'

These days I have to keep telling myself that there's often a gap between the time when God promises us a treat and when he actually gives it to us. David was anointed king years before he was actually crowned. Abraham was told to leave his city and go camping for the rest of his life because God was going to give him a son. But he had to wait twenty years until Isaac was born. I've been thinking a lot about this 'faith gap' lately and it's a very trying vacuum in which to operate. You have to hang on to the belief that God has something in store even though you haven't a clue what it is. The sight of Brodie sitting patiently by the front door really helped me. 'And we know that all that happens to us is working for our good if we love God and are fitting into his plans.' (Romans 8:28 LB)

Jenx

Dear Ell

We're here! It's not a dream, even though I do have to keep pinching myself. We moved back to the country two weeks ago. It's only a little bungalow, but it has an enchanting garden and the country here is a mass of bridleways and footpaths. There's even a blue-bell wood at the bottom of our garden. Already there are green fingers poking up through the layers of dead winter leaves promising new hope, fresh life and a new start. Brodie and I have survived the pavement years, but I've always had a nasty feeling that Labradors ought to have space to run, mud to splash through and a stream to wash in afterwards. All the same, I wouldn't have missed the last ten years because I've learnt so much. But like a Labrador, I *need* beauty and space. Something inside me has come back to life.

And Brodie? Well it's not entirely a 'happily ever after' situation for her. Everything here *ought* to be perfect, but isn't it strange that so often when all the circumstances are right, one awkward relationship can spoil it all? The proverbial fly in the ointment.

Brodie is having to adjust to another dog. No, not a puppy – a geriatric mongrel with arthritis who just happens to be deaf as well! No we're *not* starting a home for disabled dogs. The thought of doggie-sized wheelchairs whizzing about the garden is making me laugh helplessly and I just wish I could draw! No, Candy has been greatly loved by a family for fourteen years but sadly they had to leave her to live abroad. They were good friends of ours and we could not bear to see their misery at the thought of having her put to sleep. So . . . You know how these things just happen!

Brodie stayed with friends during our move and we went to fetch her a couple of days later. We collected Candy at the same time, hoping to avoid any scraps because each dog would think the other one owned the house. Candy was not deceived and instantly pulled rank while Brodie, showing due deference to age before beauty, reverted to her old place at the bottom of the family pecking order. Candy, who is a cross between a collie and a whippet, started as she meant to go on by establishing herself firmly in the best place on the hearth rug and even occupying Brodie's bed, leaving Brodie to fold herself painfully into Candy's far smaller basket.

Brodie sits about with her head cocked on one side not at all sure how to react to the invader. Her blindness means she doesn't respond to the body language which warns most dogs to tread wearily. Thus she goes blundering up to Candy, all friendly and eager to please, only to be rebuffed by a crabby snap. All the same, she keeps trying and goes back for more with her tail wagging hopefully. Her restful nature is sorely tried by Candy's restlessness. Perhaps the poor old dog is looking for her family because she patters round the house incessantly, scratching herself, sneezing, snorting and barking continuously in a deep wheezy voice, rather like a donkey with serious bronchitis. Can elderly dogs suffer from senile dementia? Her day begins about five, commencing with a volley of retching which seems to echo from various parts of the house. The routine culminates with a lengthy vomiting session while Brodie's compassion – and ours – wears rather thin. In spite of all that, Brodie is still determined to make friends. Her only sign of annoyance showed last Sunday. While we were out at church she chewed Candy's mattress to a pulp and ate half her blanket. She hasn't disgraced herself like that since puppyhood.

At the moment I've got a Candy in my life too, someone who 'barks' at all my advances and balks everything I try to do. It's *not* a member of the family, but it still makes life awkward. Perhaps we could all be saints if we lived by ourselves on desert islands! I have to confess I've reacted far less well than Brodie, and on several occasions I would cheerfully have torn up far more than a bed. Perhaps she has many more lessons to teach me about tolerance, and 'loving my neighbour'.

Poor old Candy! It's so easy to love a puppy, but when you adopt an older dog, love develops more slowly. At first I wondered what on earth we had done, but the other day while I was typing at my desk Candy came over and rested her head on my knee and looked up at me with big, sad, brown eyes. I had forgotten what it feels like to communicate with a dog by sight alone. Suddenly I thought how horrible it must be to feel abandoned by everyone you love and be forced to live with strangers who don't even like you very much. So many elderly humans must feel the same way. 'All right, Candy,' I said, 'let's be friends.'

The one thing which concerned me was that having Candy would spoil my relationship with Brodie, but I don't think it will. Candy's arthritis makes her too stiff to do more than potter round the garden, so Brodie and I have all this wonderful countryside to walk about and explore by ourselves. Brodie follows me so closely now when we are out walking. Sometimes when she was younger, particularly after Minty died, a sudden surge of youthful impetuosity would send her hurtling off on her own devices. An adolescent desire to establish her independence, perhaps? But that behaviour only caused painful knocks on the nose, so now she is quite content to trot at my heels. Wasn't it Kipling who talked about the delight of 'four feet padding behind'?

The older I get the more I realize how vital it is to walk close to God. We so nearly shot off down the wrong path over that mill house we wanted to buy in Devon. I have to admit I didn't like his sharp 'Careful!' (the word I use when Brodie is thundering in the direction of danger). Now he has brought us to this lovely place, in spite of our misplaced independence. Probably I'm every bit as blind as Brodie when it comes to finding my way through life. 'We grope about like blind people. We stumble at noon, as if it were night . . .' (Isaiah 59:10) It's a good job God can see the pitfalls coming up in the distance, just as I can see a busy road, a fast-running river or an electric fence. Staying closely at heel, that's what keeps Brodie out of trouble. The same applies to me!

The good walking weather is fast approaching; there are already primroses in the ditch down the lane. There'll be Kentish apple blossom in the orchard soon, blue flax above us on the Downs and the fields all round here will be splashed with the vivid yellow of oilseed rape. My walking boots lie by the back door and Brodie's lead is ready beside them. We can't wait.

Very much love

Jenx

P.S. This morning I woke up early and found both dogs cuddled up together on the hearth rug by the embers of last night's fire. Brodie had her head on Candy's chest, so perhaps there is hope for us all!

We want to hear from you. Please send your comments about this book to us in care of the address below. Thank you.

GRAND RAPIDS, MICHIGAN 49530 USA

WWW.ZONDERVAN.COM